A Little Book of
Scottish Baking

Marion Maxwell
Illustrated by
Catherine McWilliams

First published by The Appletree Press Ltd,
19–21 Alfred Street, Belfast, BT2 8DL.
Copyright © The Appletree Press Ltd, 1996.
Printed in the UAE. All rights reserved.

A Little Scottish Baking Book

A catalogue record for this book
is available from The British Library.

ISBN 0 86281 559 2

9 8 7 6 5 4 3 2

A Little Book of Scottish Baking

This little book aims to record the variety and richness of Scottish baking: the homely bannocks, scones and oatcakes; the sophisticated confections turned out by the ancient Incorporation of Baxters in Edinburgh; the oatmeal gingerbread of the Orkneys and the delicious breads and cakes served in Glasgow tea-rooms in the nineteenth century. Long after the arrival of the baker's cart, a love of home baking still flourishes. Here, then, are ideas aplenty if you are wanting a wee something to have with your flycup!

Buttery Rowies

No more than a mouthful each, these light and flaky yeast rolls are a breakfast speciality from Aberdeen. They are best eaten fresh, spread with butter, but they freeze well and can be reheated by toasting

450g/1lb strong plain flour	425ml/15fl oz tepid water
pinch salt	225g/8oz butter
25g/1oz fresh yeast	110g/4oz white pastry fat
1 tbsp sugar or honey	

Makes 15.

Sift flour and salt into a warm bowl. Cream yeast with sugar or honey and when frothy add to flour, together with enough water to make a medium soft dough. Mix well, cover with a damp cloth and set aside in a warm place for 30-45 minutes or until doubled in size. Cream butter and pastry fat together. Roll out the dough on a floured surface to form a long strip. Dot one-third of the butter mixture over the pastry, then fold in three as for flaky pastry and roll out again. Repeat this process twice using the remaining butter mixture. Roll out pastry and then cut out small rounds or ovals. Place on a greased and floured tray, cover again with a damp cloth and leave aside in a warm place to prove for another 30-45 minutes. Preheat oven to gas mark 6, 200°C, 400°F, and place a roasting tin half-filled with boiling water on the floor of the oven to create a moist heat. Bake for 15-20 minutes, then remove the water and bake for a further 5-10 minutes until nicely golden.

Oatcakes

Made from one of our oldest native crops, **bannocks** or oatcakes were baked on a heated hearthstone or griddle and then dried out before the fire on the "banna rack".

25g/1oz plain flour
pinch salt
pinch baking soda
110g/4oz medium oatmeal

25g/1oz butter, margarine
or bacon fat
¼ cup boiling water

Makes 4.
Sift the flour, salt and baking soda into the oatmeal. Melt the butter, margarine or fat in boiling water and add to the dry ingredients. Mix until the mixture is a spongy mass (a little extra water can be used if necessary). Turn mixture on to a surface covered with plenty of dry oatmeal and scatter more on top. Flatten the dough and roll out until ½ cm/ ¼ inch in thickness, then place a dinner plate on top and trim into a neat circle. Scatter on more oatmeal and rub it in all over the surface. Cut into quarters before baking on either a griddle or in the oven.

Griddle method: Place the oatcakes on a heated griddle or heavy pan over medium heat and bake until they dry out and curl. Then place under a grill at medium heat to cook the top of the oatcakes.

Oven method: Bake at gas mark 4, 180°C, 350°F, for 20-30 minutes or until dried out.

Aberdeen Crullas

These delicate sugary plaits are mainly associated with the fine baking traditions of Aberdeen. The name probably derives from the Gaelic word *kril*, meaning a small cake or bannock. There may also be a link with the Netherlands: *krullen* means to curl, and Dutch fish curers had frequent contact with the North-east of Scotland.

225g/8oz self-raising flour	1 egg
pinch salt	1 tbsp buttermilk (or
½ tsp ground ginger or	Greek-style yoghurt)
nutmeg	oil for frying
50g/2oz butter	icing sugar
50g/2oz caster sugar	

Makes 12.

Sift flour with salt and spice. In a separate bowl, cream the butter and sugar together. Beat in the egg, adding a little flour to prevent curdling. Stir in rest of flour, adding buttermilk to make a fairly stiff dough. Roll out thinly in a 30cm/12 inch square and cut into 12 sections approximately 10cm by 7.5cm/4 inch by 3 inch. Slice each lengthways into 3 strips, but leave the top uncut. Plait to form the crullas, then fold outer strips over the centre strip and pinch ends to seal. Fry in hot oil until golden. Drain on kitchen paper and dredge with icing sugar. Eat hot or cold.

Black Bun

This rich fruit cake was traditionally eaten on twelfth night but in later years became associated with Hogmanay.

Pastry:
350g/12oz plain flour
pinch salt
25g/1oz sugar
175g/6oz butter
6 tbsp iced water

Filling:
450g/1lb each currants and raisins
175g/6oz candied peel
225g/8oz almonds, chopped and blanched
225g/8oz plain flour
225g/8oz soft brown sugar
2 eggs, beaten
1 tsp each ground ginger, allspice and grated nutmeg
¼ tsp ground black pepper
1 tsp each cream of tartar and baking soda
75-150ml/3-5fl oz whisky or brandy
milk to bind
egg yolk to glaze

First make the pastry: sift dry ingredients, rub in butter and bind to a paste using the iced water, then rest the dough in the fridge. Preheat oven to gas mark 4, 180°C, 350°F. Grease and line a 20cm/8 inch, round cake tin. Roll out pastry thinly and use to line the tin, keeping enough for a lid. Mix all filling ingredients in a large bowl, and add enough milk to bind. Pack in mixture and seal with the lid. Prick lid all over with a fork and glaze with the egg. Make a steam slit and bake for 2 hours. Reduce heat to gas mark 1, 140°C, 275°F and bake for a further 1 hour until the top is golden. Cool before turning out.

Shortbread

Shortbread, particularly associated with Christmas and Hogmanay, is a relic of the Yule bannock - a round cake notched to suggest the sun's rays. Once made with oats, it was often set in a carved mould or strewn with caraway seeds or candied peel. There are many recipes and variations, but shortbread appears in prettiest guise as "petticoat tails", possibly from the French *petites gatelles*. It is claimed that Mary, Queen of Scots was very fond of them.

110g/4oz butter	*110g/4oz plain flour*
50g/2oz caster sugar	*50g/2oz semolina or corn flour*

Makes 1 round.

Preheat oven to gas mark 3, 160°C, 325°F. Cream butter and then beat in sugar, followed by the sifted flour and semolina. Mix until a dough is formed then roll out into a circle 18cm/7 inch in diameter. If using a mould, press dough into shape, level with a rolling pin, then turn out onto a baking tray, patterned side up. Bake for 35-45 minutes, or until pale gold in colour. Cut into triangles while still warm and dust with caster sugar.

To shape traditional petticoat tails, roll out the dough quite thinly and cut into a round, using a dinner plate. Using a tumbler, cut out a smaller cirlce from the centre. Cut remaining ring into eight sections and bake as above. To serve, set the small circle in the middle of a plate and arrange the petticoat "flounces" around it.

Flakemeal Crunchies

This is an updated version of the ever-popular oat biscuits. The coating of demerara sugar, adds a special crunch and is an inspired touch.

175g/6oz flour
1 tsp baking soda
1 tsp baking powder
175g/6oz caster sugar
110g/4oz butter
110g/4oz white pastry fat
1 egg

110g/4oz rolled oats (flake meal)
50g/2oz Weetabix, crushed
50g/2oz cornflakes, roughly crushed
50g/2oz coconut
80g/3oz demerara sugar

Makes 30.
Preheat oven to gas mark 4, 180°C, 350°F, and grease two baking trays. Sift flour, baking soda and baking powder together. Cream together caster sugar, butter and pastry fat. Add egg and mix well, then fold in flour mixture, cereals and coconut. Shape into balls the size of a large walnut and roll each in demerara sugar. Flatten into rounds, place on baking trays and bake for 20-25 minutes until golden brown.

Currant Squares

Even in the age of convenience foods, home baking skills are flourishing, though the preference has shifted from large cakes to tray bakes. Here is an unsurpassed favourite, especially when made with a delicate flaky pastry.

Flaky Pastry:	*Filling:*
140g/5oz firm butter or	*110g/4oz butter*
margarine, grated	*80g/3oz sugar*
175g/6oz flour	*225g/8oz currants*
pinch salt	*pinch spice*
iced water	*1 lemon, rind and juice*
	1 large apple, grated
	1 slice bread, crumbled

Makes 20.

To make pastry: freeze butter or margarine for half an hour before grating. Sift flour and salt, then add butter or margarine and, using a palette knife, mix into flour. Add iced water until a dough is formed. Wrap and chill in fridge. Put all filling ingredients in a saucepan and bring to boiling point. Set aside to cool. Preheat oven to gas mark 6, 200°C, 400°F. Roll out half the pastry very thinly and line a swiss roll tin. Pour on currant filling, spreading evenly, then cover with the rest of the pastry. Glaze with egg or milk and bake for 30 minutes or until light gold in colour. Dust with caster sugar and cut into squares when cool.

Almond Flory

A favourite sweet during Edinburgh's golden age, this lovely latticed tart contains a rich Florentine almond filling, flavoured with orangeflower water and laced with brandy. Serve warm with cream and a dish of thinly sliced, ice-cold oranges to cut the richness.

1 packet frozen puff pastry	80ml/3fl oz cream
Filling:	1 tbsp brandy
110g/4oz ground almonds	50g/2oz butter, softened
1 tsp orangeflower water	110g/4oz dried mixed fruit
zest of 1 lemon, grated	110g/4oz soft brown sugar
1 egg	pinch each cinnamon and
1 egg yolk	nutmeg, freshly ground

Defrost pastry and preheat oven to gas mark 7, 220°C, 425°F. Reserve enough dough for the lattice top, then roll out the pastry thinly to form a dinner plate-sized circle. Dampen a baking sheet with cold water and lay pastry circle on top. Brush around the edge with egg, then roll edges over and pinch to make a small rim. Combine the filling ingredients and spread the mixture on the pastry base. Use the reserved pastry to make a lattice top, then glaze with milk and chill in the fridge for 20 minutes. Bake for approximately 35 minutes or until nicely golden. Remove from oven and sprinkle with sugar. This tart can also be baked in a loose-bottomed flan tin if you prefer.

Whisky Tea Brack

Tea brack derives its moisture and flavour from the strong, sweet tea in which the fruit is soaked overnight. This is my version of a recipe given to the late Theodora Fitzgibbon by her grandmother who soaked the fruit in a mixture of half tea and half whisky!

225g/8oz sultanas
225g/8oz raisins
225g/8oz soft brown sugar
½ tsp cinnamon
¼ tsp grated nutmeg
2 tbsp whisky

275ml/10fl oz strong tea
450g/1lb self-raising flour
2 eggs, beaten
marmalade or honey to glaze
demerara sugar to dust

Place the sultanas, raisins, sugar, cinnamon, nutmeg, whisky and tea in a large bowl and soak overnight. Preheat oven to gas mark 3, 160°C, 325°F, and grease and line a 20cm/8 inch round cake tin. Stir in the sieved flour and eggs and mix well. Bake for approximately 1½ hours. Towards the end of baking time, brush with marmalade or honey and sprinkle with demerara sugar. To test if the brack is cooked insert a skewer into the centre, if it comes out clean then the brack is ready. When cold, slice and butter generously.

Wheaten Bannock

Before white flour became widely available and before the advent of the baker's cart, this bread would have been a mainstay of the daily diet, the buttermilk giving it added sustenance. This up-to-date version with its healthy additions couldn't be simpler to make.

110g/4oz plain white flour
3 tsp (level) baking soda
½ to ¾ tsp salt
275g/10oz coarse wholemeal flour
275g/10oz fine wholemeal flour
2 tbsp wheatgerm

80g/3oz pinhead or rolled oats
2 tbsp bran
1 tbsp (scant) brown sugar
50g/2oz butter, margarine (or 2-2½ tbsp olive oil)
825ml/1½ pt buttermilk

Makes 2.
Preheat oven to gas mark 6, 200°C, 400°F, and grease and flour two 900g/2lb loaf tins. Sieve plain flour with baking soda and salt. Stir in other dry ingredients and rub in butter or margarine (or stir in the olive oil.) Gradually add the buttermilk until the mixture is slack enough to spoon into the tins. Place in the oven and bake for 50-60 minutes. To test if the wheaten is cooked through, tap on the bottom, if it sounds hollow it is ready. Cover with a cloth until cold. This bread freezes well.

Buttermilk Scones

Morning coffee and afternoon tea would not be complete without fresh scones and there are so many delicious varieties. The secret of making good scones is a quick, light hand when mixing and a hot oven.

225g/8oz self-raising soda-bread flour
pinch salt
25g/1oz butter or hard margarine

1 egg, beaten
140ml/5fl oz buttermilk
egg or milk to glaze (optional)

Makes 8.

Preheat oven to gas mark 8, 230°C, 450°F. Sift flour with salt and rub in butter or margarine. Make a well in the centre and pour in the egg and most of the buttermilk. Mix quickly to form a soft dough, adding a little extra buttermilk if necessary. Turn out on to a floured surface and roll out lightly until 2.5cm/1 inch in thickness. Working quickly, cut into 5cm/2 inch rounds. Glaze with egg or milk and set on a floured baking sheet. Bake for 15-20 minutes until light brown.

Savoury Cheese and Herb Scones

Add 1tsp dry mustard, 50g (2oz) grated cheese and 2 tbsp fresh, chopped herbs to the dry ingredients and proceed as before. After brushing with egg or milk, scatter a little grated cheese on the top of each scone.

Broonie

This is a traditional oatmeal gingerbread from Orkney. In her book, *The Scots Kitchen*, Marian Mc Neill recalls being offered some as a child by a friend who had brought it as her school "piece". The name comes from the old Norse word *bruni*, meaning a thick bannock.

175g/6oz plain flour	175g/6oz medium oatmeal
pinch salt	2 tbsp (heaped) butter
1 tsp (level) baking powder	2 tbsp treacle or molasses
110g/4oz soft brown sugar	1 egg, beaten
1 tsp (heaped) ground ginger	275ml/10fl oz buttermilk

Makes 8.

Preheat oven to gas mark 4, 180°C, 350°F. Sift flour with salt, baking powder, brown sugar and ginger and stir into oatmeal. Rub in the butter. In a separate bowl melt the treacle and blend with the egg and most of the buttermilk. Add the liquid to the oatmeal mixture and stir well. Add enough buttermilk to make the mixture a dropping consistency. Turn into a greased 900g/2lb loaf tin and bake for about 1¼ hours or until well risen. Do not cut until quite cold.

Scripture Cake

This delicious fruit cake is perfect for Sunday tea and for entertaining visitors. The recipe is cleverly devised to send you thumbing through your bible to decipher the ingredients. The results, of course, are divine!

110g/4oz Jeremiah Ch. I v. 11
340g/12oz Jeremiah Ch. XXIV v. 2
340g/12oz I Chronicles Ch. XII v. 40
500g/1lb 2oz Leviticus Ch. II v. 2
2 tsp (level) Galacians Ch. V v. 9
1 tsp (level) Solomon Ch. IV v. 14
pinch St. Matthew Ch.V v. 13
6 Job Ch.XXXIX v. 14
340g/12oz Isaiah Ch. VII v. 15
450g/1lb Jeremiah Ch. VI v. 20
½ breakfast cup Solomon Ch. IV v. 11
2 tbsp I Samuel Ch. XIV v. 29

Preheat oven to gas mark 3, 180°C, 350°F, and grease and line a 22cm/9 inch cake tin. Blanch, peel and chop the almonds. Chop the figs. Sift flour with baking powder, cinnamon and salt. Cream butter and caster sugar until fluffy. Gradually mix in beaten eggs, adding a little flour with each addition. Fold in the rest of the flour along with the honey, milk and fruit. Turn into tin and bake for approximately 2¼ hours. The cake is ready when a skewer is inserted and comes out clean.

Tattie Scones

Made from leftover potatoes, these are delicious eaten straight from the frying pan spread with plenty of butter and sometimes with sugar, syrup or honey. They are also popular fried with a cooked breakfast.

225g/8oz warm cooked potato
½ tsp salt
25g/1oz butter, melted
50g/2oz plain flour

Makes 8.
Mash potatoes well. Add salt and butter, then work in enough flour to make a pliable dough. Divide the dough in two and roll out on a floured surface to form two circles 22cm/9 inch in diameter and ½cm/¼ inch in thickness. Cut each circle into quarters and bake on a hot griddle or pan for about 5 minutes or until browned on both sides. Some people like to grease the baking surface, while others prefer a light dusting of flour for a drier effect.

Baps

The bap is the traditional morning roll of Scotland, eaten soft, floury and warm from the oven. In the sixteenth century, a "bawbee bap" was one that sold for a halfpenny. Writing in 1955, author Victor MacClure recalls "having it stuffed with Ayrshire bacon and a fried egg to eat while hastening to beat the bell for morning school."

450g/1lb plain flour, warmed
1 tsp salt
50g/2oz lard

25g/1oz fresh yeast
1 tsp sugar
275ml/10fl oz tepid milk and water mixed

Makes 8.

Sift flour and salt into a warmed bowl. Lightly rub in lard. Cream yeast with sugar and mix with most of liquid. Mix into flour, adding remaining liquid as necessary, and knead lightly to form a soft dough. Cover with a damp cloth and leave in a warm place to rise for 1-1½ hours. Turn out on to a floured surface, knead lightly again, then form into oval shapes about 11cm by 7.5cm/4½ inch by 3 inch. Set well apart on a floured baking sheet then cover and set aside for 15 minutes. Preheat oven to gas mark 7, 220°C, 425°F. Brush baps with milk and sprinkle with flour. Press your finger into each bap (to prevent it blistering when cooking) and bake for 15-20 minutes. Dust with a little flour if liked.

Barley Bannocks

Leeze me on thee, John Barleycorn,
Thou king o' grain!
On thee auld Scotland chaws her cood
In souple scones, the wale o' food.

Thus Robert Burns pays tribute to the fact that barley was, along with oats, the staple grain of Scotland in ancient times. This recipe is the kind of bread that was made daily on the girdle or, more primitively, on a heated hearthstone. Tradition has it that kneading should be done "sunwise", with a right-handed turn.

450g/1lb barley meal	*1 tsp salt*
110g/4oz plain flour	*2 tsp baking soda*
2 tsp cream of tartar	*550ml/1 pint buttermilk*

Makes 4.

Sieve barley meal and flour together with cream of tartar and salt. Stir soda into buttermilk and when it fizzes, pour it into the flour mixture. Mix to a soft dough, using a little extra flour if necessary. Turn out on to a floured surface and roll out lightly until 3cm/1½ inch thick. Cut into rounds or divide into farls. Set on a hot girdle or electric pan and bake until underside is brown. Turn and brown on other side.

Seed Cake

For centuries, caraway seeds have been used to lend a distinctive flavour to puddings, biscuits and cakes. A handful would often be thrown in to speckle a sweetened soda bread. This rich cake, known also as "carvie", recalls days of gracious living in substantial country houses, when visiting ladies would be offered a slice with a glass of port.

275g/10oz flour	225g/8oz butter
½ tsp baking powder	225g/8oz caster sugar
¼ tsp cinnamon	4 eggs, beaten
¼ tsp nutmeg	3 tbsp caraway seeds

Preheat oven to gas mark 3, 160°C, 325°F, and grease and line a 20cm/8 inch cake tin. Sift flour with baking powder, cinnamon and nutmeg. In a separate bowl, cream the butter and sugar together until pale and fluffy, then gradually mix in the eggs, adding a little flour with each addition. Fold in the rest of the flour and mix well. Reserve a teaspoon of the caraway seeds to decorate the top of the cake and stir the rest into the mixture. Bake for approximately 1½ hours, until pale gold in colour and firm to the touch.

Lila's Apple Tart

This is how the best baker in my neighbourhood makes this universal family favourite. It combines the tartness of Bramleys, a couple of Cox's Pippins and, following the old books, a quince for superb flavour.

Shortcrust Pastry:
8oz/225g self raising flour
pinch salt
2oz/50g white pastry fat
2oz/50g good quality margarine
1 egg, beaten

Filling:
450g/1lb Bramley apples, peeled, cored and thinly sliced
225g/8oz Cox's Pippins, peeled, cored and thinly sliced
1 quince, grated (optional)
3 tbsp (heaped) sugar
nutmeg or cloves, grated
caster sugar to dust

To make the pastry: Sift the flour and salt into a large mixing bowl. Cut the fat and margarine into small cubes and rub into the flour until the mixture resembles breadcrumbs. Mix the egg with a little water, reserve some to use as a glaze, and use the rest to bind the flour into a dough. Then wrap and chill in the fridge for 30 minutes. Preheat oven to gas mark 6, 200°C, 400°F, warm a baking sheet, and grease and line a 24cm/9 inch pie dish. Roll out a little more than half the pastry on a floured surface and line the pie dish. Place apples and quince (if using) into the dish and add sugar and a little freshly grated nutmeg or cloves. Roll out the rest of the pastry to form a lid. Brush the rim of the pastry base with water and place the lid on top. Seal and flute edges and make a few slits in the lid to allow steam to escape. Glaze with reserved egg and sprinkle with caster sugar. Place pie dish on the warmed baking sheet and bake for 30 minutes. Serve with cream.

Parlies

These cakes are said to have been popular with members of the Scottish parliament. Golden syrup - itself, incidentally, the invention of a Scottish sugar firm - can be used instead of treacle. Though it's not traditional, you could ice your parlies with a dab of orange-flavoured water icing, topped with a sliver of crystallised ginger.

> 50g/2oz caster sugar
> 110g/4oz butter or margarine
> 225g/8oz flour
> 1 tsp ground ginger
> 1 small egg
> 2 tbsp treacle, warmed

Preheat oven to gas mark 4, 180°C, 350°F. Cream sugar and butter together until fluffy. Sift flour with ginger. Stir egg into treacle and add, along with the flour, to the creamed butter. Drop dessertspoonfuls of the mixture on to a greased baking sheet, leaving room for spreading. Bake for 15-20 minutes until golden. Cool on a rack.

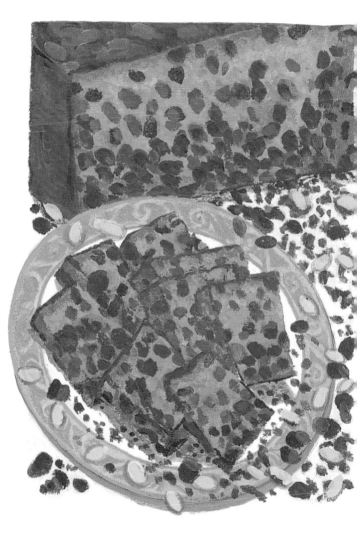

Dundee Cake

Dundee cake, with its distinctive topping of blanched almonds, has drawn world-wide attention to the excellence of Scotland's baking tradition. With its good keeping qualities it makes a perfect special occasion cake.

225g/8oz plain flour, sifted
1 tsp (level) baking powder
140g/5oz butter
140g/5oz caster sugar
3 large eggs, beaten
2 tbsp brandy (optional)
2 tbsp milk
340g/12oz dried mixed fruit
50g/2oz chopped candied peel
2 tbsp ground almonds
1 tsp each fresh orange and lemon zest
50g/2oz glace cherries (optional)
50g/2oz whole blanched almonds

Preheat oven to gas mark 3, 170°C, 325°F, and grease and line a 20cm/8 inch round cake tin. Sift flour with baking powder. Cream butter and sugar together until pale and fluffy. Beat in the eggs a little at a time, stirring in a little flour with each addition. Fold in the remaining flour, adding brandy if using and stirring in a little milk, if necessary, to achieve a soft dropping consistency. Gently fold in dried fruit, peel, ground almonds, citrus zest and cherries, if using. Turn into tin and smooth top. Arrange almonds on top and bake for 2-2½ hours. Best matured for a few days before cutting.

Chocolate Whisky Cake

Every baker's repertoire will include a favourite recipe for chocolate cake. Lending a distinctive Scottish flavour to this one is a smooth whisky icing. There is also a surprise ingredient in the cake itself which contributes to its wonderful moist texture. See if your guests can identify what it is!

Sponge:
175g/6oz self-raising flour
½ tsp salt
50g/2oz dark chocolate
110g/4oz butter
175g/6oz caster sugar
80g/3oz cooked mashed potato

2 eggs, beaten
4 tbsp milk
Filling:
110g/4oz dark chocolate
125ml/4fl oz double cream
50g/2oz icing sugar
3 tbsp whisky

Preheat oven to gas mark 5, 190°C, 375°F, and grease and-line two 20cm/8 inch cake tins. Sift flour and salt into a mixing bowl. Melt chocolate in a bowl placed over a saucepan of hot water. In a separate bowl, cream butter and sugar together until fluffy, then beat in the chocolate and mashed potato. Beat in the eggs, adding a little flour with each addition. Fold in the rest of flour and stir in the milk. Divide mixture between cake tins and bake for 25-30 minutes. Remove from oven and after a few minutes, turn out on to a cooling rack. While the cake is cooling make the filling. Melt the chocolate as before, stir in the other ingredients and mix. Use the filling to sandwich the sponge layers together and coat the top and sides of the cake.

Scottish Pancakes

Add these airy little pancakes to your repertoire and you'll never be lost for something hot and fresh to offer to unexpected guests. Ready in minutes, they are delicious spread with lemon curd.

110g/4oz self-raising flour
½ tsp baking powder
1 dsp sugar
1 tbsp cooking oil or melted butter
1 egg, beaten
175ml/6 fl oz milk

Makes 10.

Sift flour and baking powder into a large mixing bowl. Add the sugar and stir in the butter or oil, egg and most of the milk, and mix well. Add the remaining milk until the mixture is a thick, smooth batter able to hold its shape when dropped in little rounds on a griddle or pan. When bubbles appear on the surface turn over and cook the other side. (It is a good idea to make a trial scone to test the temperature of the griddle.) When cooked, the scones should be golden brown and spongy inside.

Country Rhubarb Cake

In the early eighteenth century, the Duke of Atholl had a famous "Turkey rhubarb" plantation at Blair Castle, from which he supplied an eminent Edinburgh druggist with rhubarb roots for grinding up as a purgative.

Scone dough:
340g/12oz plain flour
½ tsp baking soda
pinch salt
50g/2oz caster sugar
80g/3oz butter
1 egg

175ml/6fl oz buttermilk
Filling:
700g/1½lb rhubarb, roughly chopped
200-250g/7-9oz sugar
white of 1 egg, whisked
caster sugar to dust

Preheat oven to gas mark 4, 180°C, 350°F, and grease a 25cm/10 inch deep pie dish. Sieve flour, baking soda and salt into a mixing bowl. Add caster sugar and rub in butter. In a separate bowl, beat the egg together with the buttermilk and gradually add this to the flour until a dough is formed. Knead lightly on a floured surface and divide dough into two. Roll out one half and use it to line the pie dish. Fill the dish with the rhubarb and sprinkle with the sugar (the quantity required depends on the tartness of the rhubarb). Roll out the remaining dough to form a pastry lid. Brush the rim of the pastry base with water and put on the lid. Glaze with the whisked egg white and sprinkle with caster sugar. Make steam slits in the lid and bake for 50-60 minutes or until the crust is lightly browned and the fruit is soft. This pie is also delicious if made with apples.

Selkirk Bannock

This round, yeasted fruit loaf was made famous in Scotland in the mid-nineteenth century by Robbie Douglas in his bakery in Selkirk Market Place. Reputedly, it was the only thing that Queen Victoria ate when she visited Sir Walter Scott's granddaughter at Abbotsford in 1869.

110g/4oz butter	¼ tsp salt
110g/4oz lard	450g/1lb sultanas
275ml/10fl oz milk, warmed	110g/4oz chopped peel
	225g/8oz caster sugar
25g/1oz fresh yeast	1 tbsp each warm milk
½ tsp sugar	and sugar mixed to glaze
900g/2lb strong plain flour	

Warm all the ingredients and utensils. Soften the butter and lard, then stir in the warmed milk. Cream yeast with the sugar and add to mixture. Sift flour and salt, pour in the liquid and form a dough. Knead on a floured surface for 10 minutes, then return to the bowl. Enclose in a polythene bag and leave in a warm place until doubled in size. Knead until smooth, add fruit and caster sugar and knead again for about 5 minutes. Shape into a flat round approximately 23cm/9 inch in diameter and place on a greased baking sheet. Cover again and set in a warm place for 35-40 minutes. Bake at gas mark 5, 190°C, 350°F for 60-75 minutes. A little before the end of baking time, glaze the bannock. When cooked, the bannock will sound hollow when tapped on the bottom.

Sair Heidies

A testimony to the Scottish sense of humour, these "sore heads" used to be popular in Grampian bakeries. The straight-sided cakes are wrapped in paper "bandages" and have domed heads crusted with crushed lump sugar representing "aspirin"! They are traditionally baked in special rings, but you can improvise by using metal pastry cutters, or even muffin tins.

140g/5oz self-raising flour
50g/2oz margarine
50g/2oz caster sugar

2 eggs
crushed lump sugar to decorate

Preheat oven to gas mark 6, 200°C, 400°F. Using greaseproof paper or firm writing paper, cut out ten paper jackets, 16cm by 4.5cm/6½ by 2 inch. Brush both sides of the jackets with oil, then set rings on a baking tray and line with the jackets. Whisk all ingredients for buns together thoroughly and spoon into the rings. Sprinkle with crushed sugar. Bake for about 15 minutes. Leave to cool for a few minutes, then ease out of rings.

Scottish Snowballs

A universal favourite in home bakeries, there are no prizes for guessing how these buns get their name. They bear, however, only a passing resemblance to the "snow cake", a sweet, white cake made with arrowroot and egg whites, for which Mrs. Beeton gives a "genuine Scotch recipe".

225g/8oz flour	1 egg
80g/3oz caster sugar	1 egg yolk
pinch salt	225g/8oz icing sugar
80g/3oz margarine	50g/2oz dessicated coconut

Makes 10.

Preheat oven to gas mark 6, 200°C, 400°F. Stir flour, caster sugar and salt together. Rub in the margarine and then bind to a stiff dough using the egg and egg yolk. Turn out on to a floured surface and press into a flat cake. Cut in quarters and divide each into five pieces. Roll each piece into a ball and arrange on a greased baking tray. Bake for 15 minutes, then leave to cool. Mix together half the icing sugar and 1 dsp water to make a stiff icing and use to sandwich the cakes in pairs. Mix remaining icing sugar with 3 dsp water to make a thinner icing and dip the cakes into this before rolling in coconut and drying in bun trays.

Boiled Fruit Cake

With the ingredients measured out in cupfuls (a standard breakfast cup will do) and no creaming or rubbing in to be done, this cut-and-come-again cake is an established favourite.

1 cup water	*1¼ cups sultanas*
225g/8oz butter	*¼ cup cherries*
1 cup soft brown sugar	*1 tsp mixed spice*
½ cup peel	*2 cups flour*
1½ cups raisins	*1 tsp baking soda*
	2 eggs, beaten

Put first eight ingredients into a large saucepan and bring to a boil. Simmer gently for 20 minutes, then set aside to cool. Preheat oven to gas mark 4, 180°C, 350°F, and grease and line a 20cm/8 inch cake tin. Sieve the flour and baking soda into the fruit mixture and add the beaten eggs. Mix well, then turn into a cake tin and bake for 1-1½ hours or until cooked through. (Reduce the temperature towards the end of the cooking time if necessary.) Cool in the tin for 15 minutes, then turn out on to a rack. This cake will keep well if stored in an airtight tin.

Featherlight Sponge Cake

This light-as-air cake is often used as a yardstick for judging the best baker in the parish, some of whom will swear by using duck eggs for extra volume. Perfect simply sandwiched with jam and cream, this basic mixture can also be transformed into a swiss roll, a layered gateau or a trifle base.

4 large eggs, separated
4oz/110g caster sugar
4oz/110g self-raising flour, sieved

Preheat oven to gas mark 4, 180°C, 350°F, and grease and line two 18cm/7 inch cake tins. Beat egg yolks and sugar together until very pale and thick, then set aside. In a separate bowl, beat the egg whites until they stand in stiff peaks. Fold the egg whites into the egg and sugar mixture, then gently fold in the flour. Divide the mixture between the cake tins and bake in the middle of the oven for about 25-30 minutes, until the sponge has shrunk slightly from the sides of the tins and is firm and springy to the touch. When cold, sandwich together with jam, cream, fresh fruit, lemon curd or a combination of these. Finish with a dusting of caster sugar, or make a pretty pattern by sprinkling icing sugar over a doily set on the cake.

Index